CLIMATE CHANGE

IN INFOGRAPHICS

Enviro Graphics

CHERRY LAKE PRESS

Published in the United States of America by Cherry Lake Publishing Group
Ann Arbor, Michigan
www.cherrylakepublishing.com

Reading Adviser: Marla Conn, MS, Ed., Literacy specialist, Read-Ability, Inc.
Photo Credits: ©OpenClipart-Vectors/Pixabay, cover; ©Shutterstock, cover; ©Shutterstock, cover;
©Shutterstock, 1; ©Shutterstock, 4; ©Shutterstock, 7; ©Clker-Free-Vector-Images/Pixabay, 8;
©CoxinhaFotos/Pixabay, 8; ©Clker-Free-Vector-Images/Pixabay, 8; ©Juhele/Pixabay, 8; ©Shutterstock,
8; ©OpenClipart-Vectors/Pixabay, 9; ©OpenClipart-Vectors/Pixabay, 9; ©JerzyGorecki/Pixabay,
9; ©OpenClipart-Vectors/Pixabay, 9; ©OpenClipart-Vectors/Pixabay, 9; ©CoxinhaFotos/Pixabay,
15; ©Shutterstock, 15; ©Shutterstock, 15; ©Juliemac814/Pixabay, 16; ©Clker-Free-Vector-Images/
Pixabay, 16; ©OpenClipart-Vectors/Pixabay, 16; ©OpenClipart-Vectors/Pixabay, 16; ©Clker-
Free-Vector-Images/Pixabay, 16; ©Clker-Free-Vector-Images/Pixabay, 18; ©vasil360/Pixabay,
18; ©Clker-Free-Vector-Images/Pixabay, 18; ©Shutterstock, 18; ©Clker-Free-Vector-Images/
Pixabay, 19; ©vasil360/Pixabay, 19; ©Clker-Free-Vector-Images/Pixabay, 19; ©Shutterstock, 19;
©Shutterstock, 19; ©Clker-Free-Vector-Images/Pixabay, 23; ©JerzyGorecki/Pixabay, 25; ©Clker-
Free-Vector-Images/Pixabay, 27; ©Pixaline/Pixabay, 27; ©Shutterstock, 27; ©Shutterstock, 30

Cherry Lake Press is an imprint of Cherry Lake Publishing Group.

Library of Congress Cataloging-in-Publication Data has been filed and is available at catalog.loc.gov

Cherry Lake Publishing Group would like to acknowledge the work of the
Partnership for 21st Century Learning, a Network of Battelle for Kids. Please
visit http://www.battelleforkids.org/networks/p21 for more information.

Printed in the United States of America
Corporate Graphics

TABLE OF CONTENTS

What Is Climate Change?

The climate is always changing. This happens naturally. It takes thousands of years. Humans can change the climate too. They do it much more quickly than nature. The climate has changed in at least the past 140 years. Average temperatures are getting hotter. Sea levels are rising. Many scientists are worried about how this will affect the world. Understanding climate change can help people make different choices. They can reduce their impact.

WEATHER VS. CLIMATE

Weather		Climate
Measured in days and weeks	VS.	Measured in decades
Day-to-day information	VS.	At least 30 years of information
Describes a small area	VS.	Refers to a large area
Easier to predict	VS.	Harder to predict
Looks at temperature, **precipitation**, and wind	VS.	Looks at average temperatures, sea level, and frequency of extreme weather

CHAPTER 1

Causes of Climate Change

Climate change happens because of changes in Earth's energy balance. Life needs some heat. Heat comes from the sun. It gets trapped by the **atmosphere**. If too much heat is trapped, Earth's surface can get too hot. This is called the Greenhouse Effect. If too much heat escapes, it can get too cold. Other factors can skew Earth's energy balance too.

EARTH'S ENERGY BALANCE

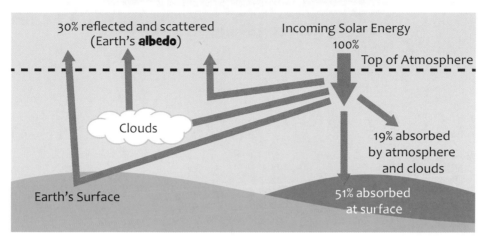

30% reflected and scattered
(Earth's **albedo**)

Incoming Solar Energy
100%

Top of Atmosphere

Clouds

19% absorbed
by atmosphere
and clouds

Earth's Surface

51% absorbed
at surface

TRAPPING HEAT

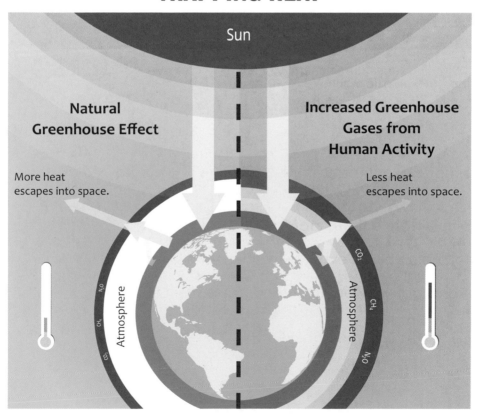

Sun

Natural
Greenhouse Effect

Increased Greenhouse
Gases from
Human Activity

More heat
escapes into space.

Less heat
escapes into space.

Atmosphere

Atmosphere

CONTRIBUTIONS TO THE GREENHOUSE EFFECT

Natural

Plants and animals

Volcanoes

Asteroids

Human-caused

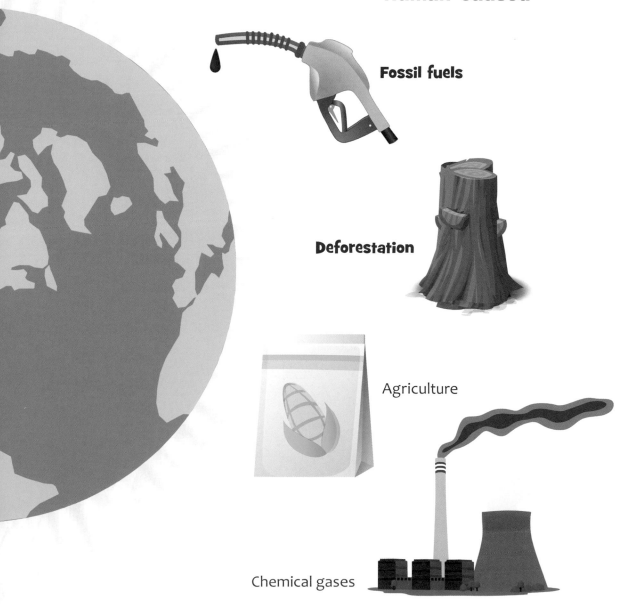

Fossil fuels

Deforestation

Agriculture

Chemical gases

GREENHOUSE GASES FROM HUMANS

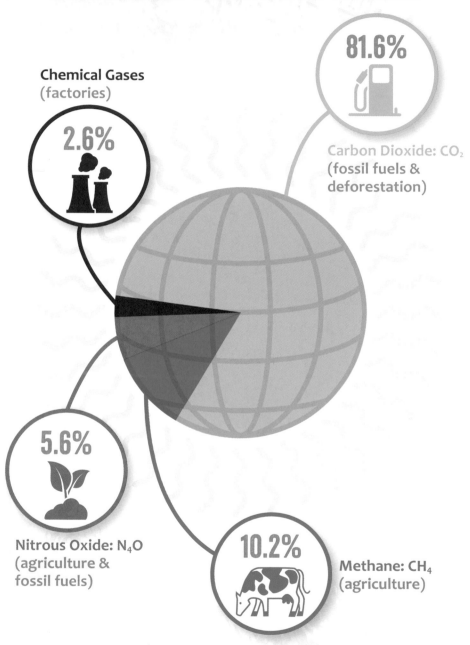

81.6%

Carbon Dioxide: CO_2
(fossil fuels &
deforestation)

Chemical Gases
(factories)

2.6%

5.6%

Nitrous Oxide: N_4O
(agriculture &
fossil fuels)

10.2%

Methane: CH_4
(agriculture)

2017, U.S. Environmental Protection Agency (EPA)

CO$_2$ EMISSIONS BY HUMANS

Emissions are gases and particles that are put into the air. Emissions pollute the air and add to climate change.

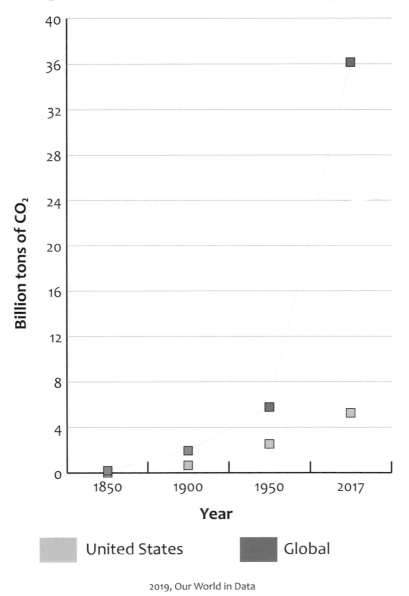

Year

United States   Global

2019, Our World in Data

U.S. VEHICLE EMISSIONS

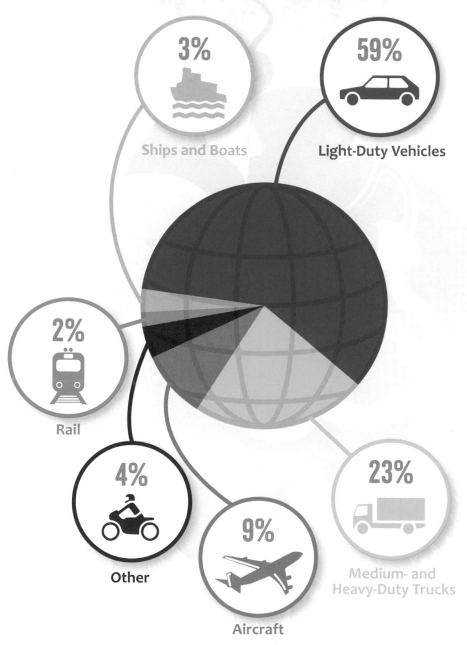

3%
Ships and Boats

59%
Light-Duty Vehicles

2%
Rail

4%
Other

9%
Aircraft

23%
Medium- and
Heavy-Duty Trucks

2017, EPA

EMISSIONS Q&A

Using 1 gallon (3.8 liters) of gas in a passenger car creates how much emissions?

20 pounds (9 kilograms) of CO_2

Driving a passenger car for 1 year creates how much emissions?

About 5 tons of CO_2

Do cars emit other greenhouse gases?

Yes. Methane and nitrous oxide come from tailpipes. Air conditioners can leak gases too.

2018, EPA

CHAPTER 2

Effects of Climate Change

Human activity is speeding up climate change. Many natural systems are changing. These changes are happening quickly. It can be hard for plants and animals to keep up. Plants and animals need each other to live. When one species becomes **extinct**, that can make it harder for other plants and animals to survive. They eventually become extinct too.

EFFECTS OF CLIMATE CHANGE

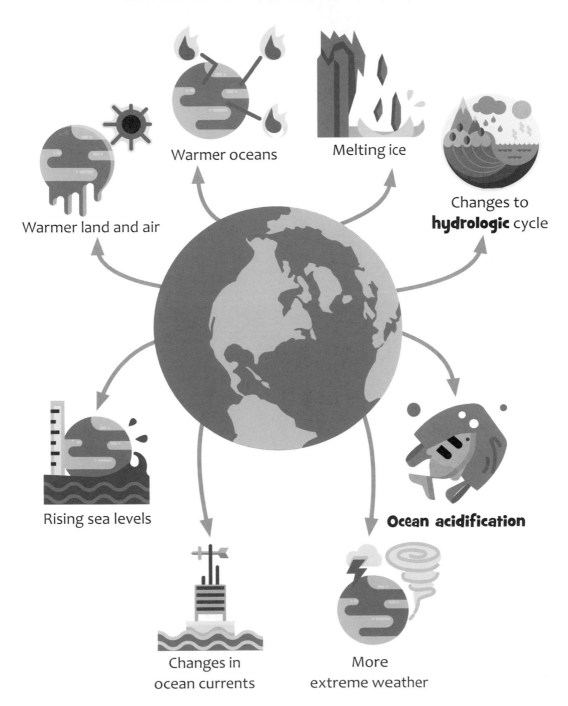

Warmer land and air

Warmer oceans

Melting ice

Changes to **hydrologic** cycle

Rising sea levels

Changes in ocean currents

More extreme weather

Ocean acidification

ANIMALS THREATENED BY CLIMATE CHANGE

BEES AND OTHER INSECTS
Food and habitats
are being lost due to
rising temperatures.

WHALES AND SHARKS
Warming oceans disrupt
normal life.

ELEPHANTS
Changing weather
patterns disturb these
sensitive creatures.

GIRAFFES
Main plant food is
dying off due to
warmer temperatures.

OCEAN BIRDS
Rising sea levels
destroy
nesting grounds.

NUMBER OF EXTINCTIONS AND HUMANS

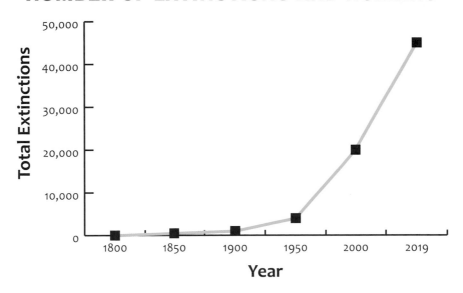

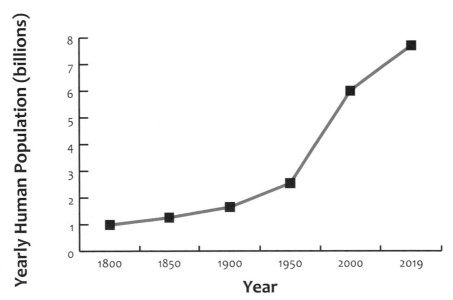

*The two charts show a strong **correlation**. This does not necessarily mean a cause-and-effect relationship.*

2008, U.S. Geological Survey; 2018, Our World in Data

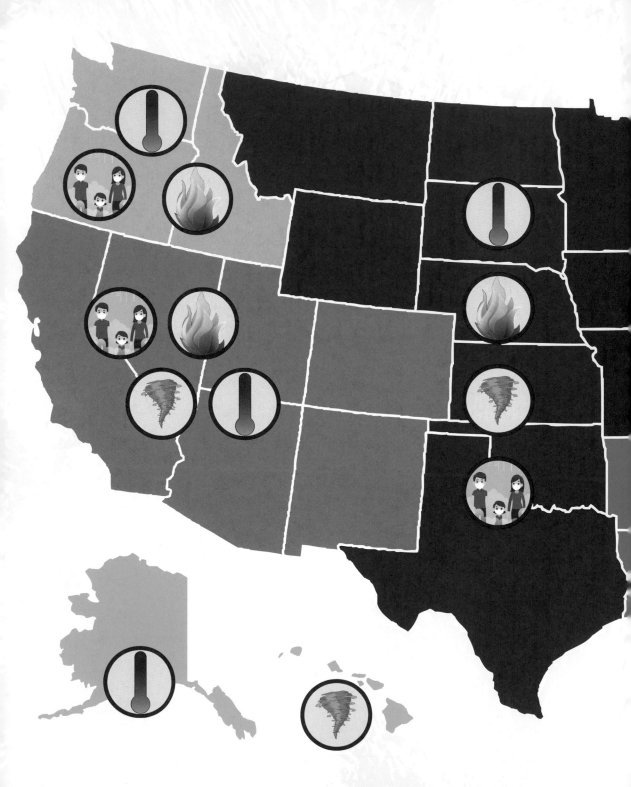

HOW HUMANS ARE THREATENED BY CLIMATE CHANGE

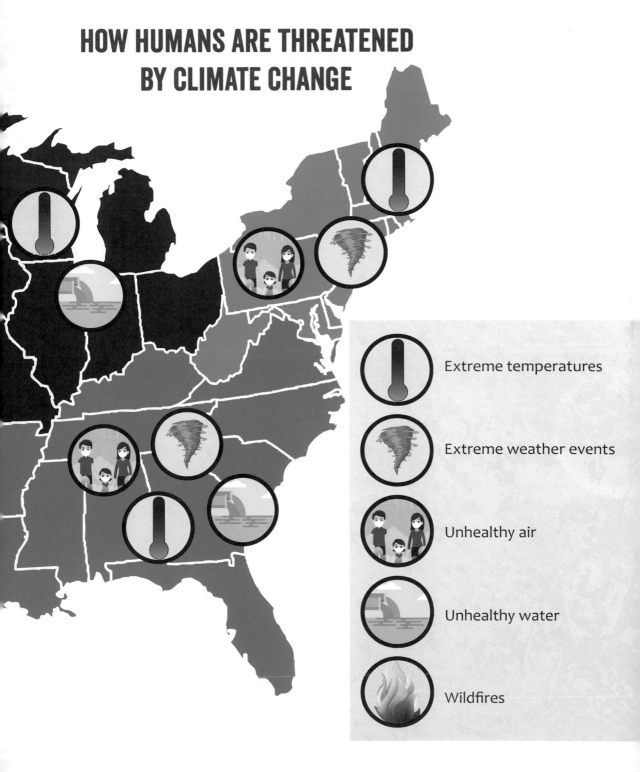

Extreme temperatures

Extreme weather events

Unhealthy air

Unhealthy water

Wildfires

SEA LEVEL RISE

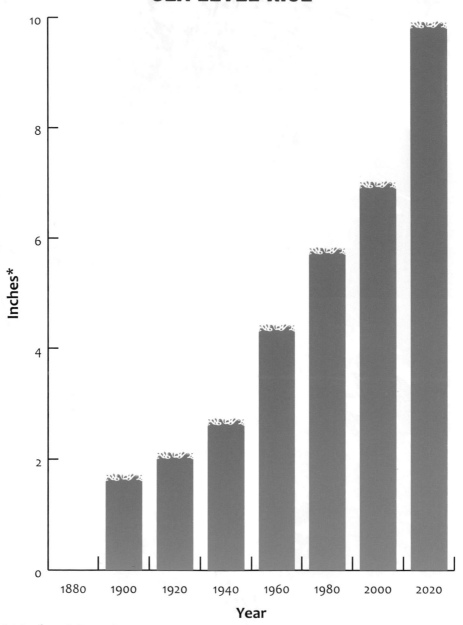

*1 inch = 2.5 centimeters

2020, NASA Jet Propulsion Laboratory

STATES MOST AT RISK OF SEA LEVEL RISE

FLORIDA

8,436
COASTLINE MILES*

15 MILLION
COASTAL POPULATION

CALIFORNIA

3,427
COASTLINE MILES

26 MILLION
COASTAL POPULATION

WASHINGTON

3,026
COASTLINE MILES

5 MILLION
COASTAL POPULATION

1 mile = 1.6 kilometers

NEW YORK

2,625
COASTLINE MILES

16 MILLION
COASTAL POPULATION

2016, National Oceanic and Atmospheric Administration (NOAA); 2019, NOAA

CHAPTER 3

Human Response

Since 1880, the average global temperature has gone up. It has risen by about 1.4 degrees Fahrenheit (0.8 degrees Celsius). Scientists think a rise of more than 2.7°F (1.5°C) may not be safe. People are looking toward the future. If action is taken now, climate change can be reduced. If people and countries do not change, life on Earth will change forever.

AVERAGE WARMING BY 2100

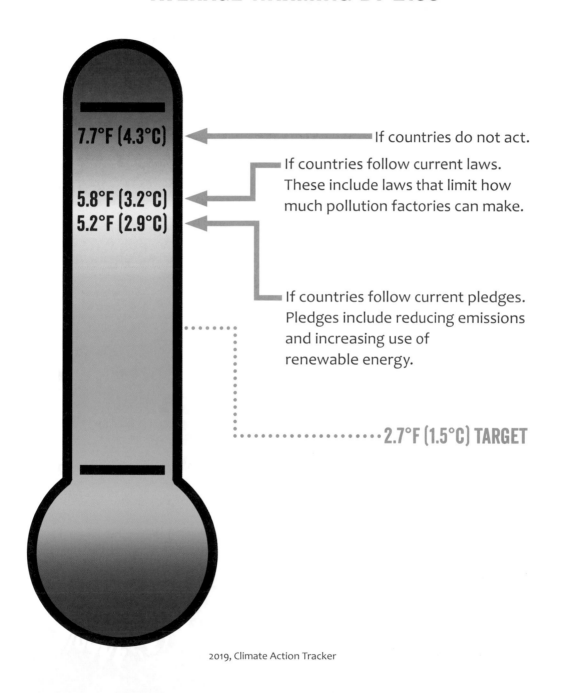

7.7°F (4.3°C) — If countries do not act.

5.8°F (3.2°C) — If countries follow current laws. These include laws that limit how much pollution factories can make.

5.2°F (2.9°C) — If countries follow current pledges. Pledges include reducing emissions and increasing use of renewable energy.

2.7°F (1.5°C) TARGET

2019, Climate Action Tracker

TIMELINE

1800s
Human population booms. Emissions increase too.

1930s
Scientists first report a global warming trend.

1970s
Oil prices go way up. This draws attention to fossil fuels. Many people start to worry about climate change.

2000s
Scientists find climate change is hard to predict. Many people debate the issue of climate change.

2015
Many countries sign the Paris Agreement. They agree to lower emissions.

2019
Temperatures and CO2 levels are among the highest ever recorded.

GLOBAL EMISSIONS BY 2030

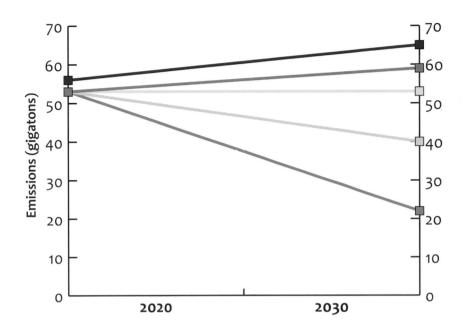

If no actions are taken, global emissions will keep going up and average warming will keep increasing.

If all current plans to reduce emissions and use renewable energy are followed, global emissions will still keep going up as countries continue to grow.

If Paris Agreement pledges are followed, global emissions will stay about the same.

To keep average warming below 35.6°F (2°C), emissions must be reduced further.

To keep average warming below 34.7°F (1.5°C), emissions must be reduced by at least 55 percent.

2018, United Nations Environment Programme

VEHICLES IN THE UNITED STATES

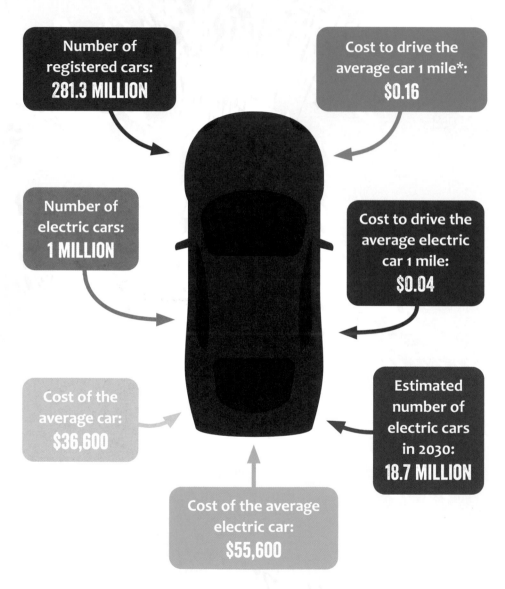

Number of registered cars:
281.3 MILLION

Cost to drive the average car 1 mile*:
$0.16

Number of electric cars:
1 MILLION

Cost to drive the average electric car 1 mile:
$0.04

Cost of the average car:
$36,600

Estimated number of electric cars in 2030:
18.7 MILLION

Cost of the average electric car:
$55,600

*1 mile = 1.6 kilometers

2019 Kelley Blue Book; 2019, U.S. Department of Energy; 2018, Edison Electric Institute; 2011, Idaho National Laboratory

VEHICLE SOLUTIONS

Solution 1

Drive cars that are more fuel efficient. Less fuel means less emissions.

Solution 2

Use cleaner fuel. Certain **biofuels** reduce emissions by 80 percent.

Solution 3

Drive electric cars and trucks. All-electric vehicles have zero emissions.

REDUCING YOUR EFFECT ON CLIMATE CHANGE

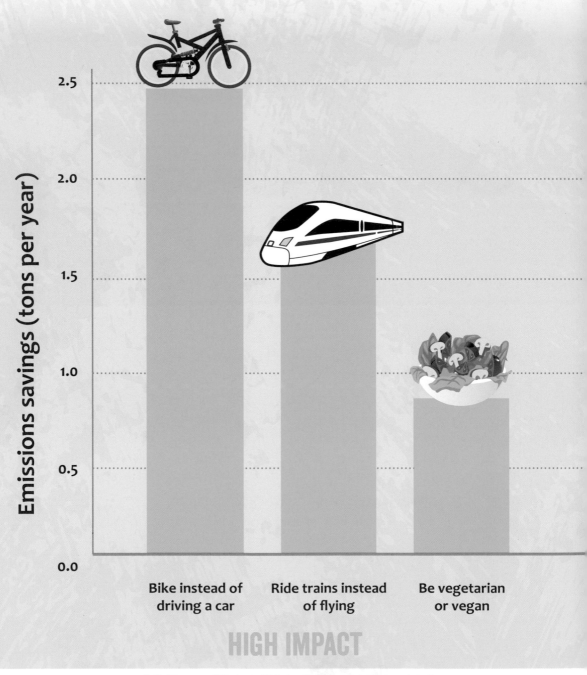

Emissions savings (tons per year)

2.5
2.0
1.5
1.0
0.5
0.0

Bike instead of driving a car

Ride trains instead of flying

Be vegetarian or vegan

HIGH IMPACT

2017, Seth Wynes and Kimberly Nicholas, Environmental Research Letters

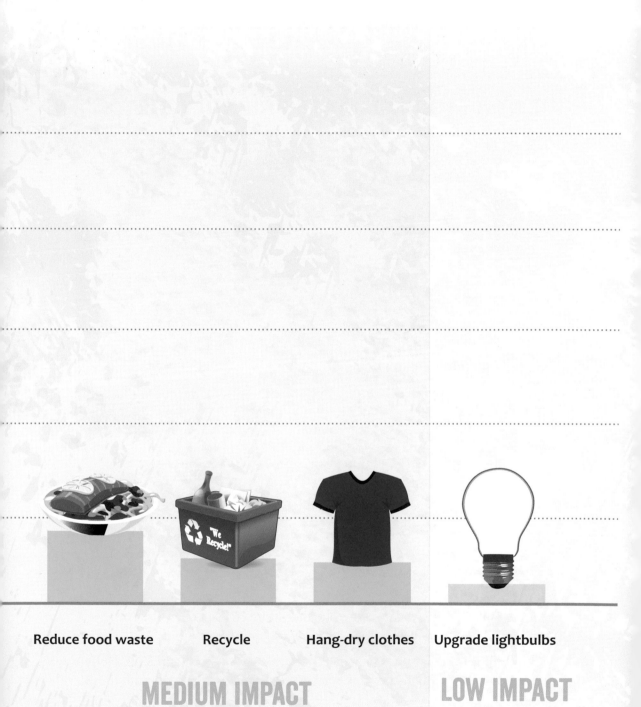

Reduce food waste   Recycle   Hang-dry clothes   Upgrade lightbulbs

MEDIUM IMPACT   LOW IMPACT

EAT A MORE CLIMATE-FRIENDLY DIET

Your diet can have a large impact on climate change. There are many ways to reduce your effect.

1. For one day, keep a log of everything you eat. Write down what you eat at each meal.

2. Research where the food came from. Was it grown locally? Did it come from a different country? How far did it travel to get to your plate?

3. Brainstorm ways to make your diet more climate friendly. Some ideas are to eat less meat and grow your own vegetables.

4. Talk to your family. See what changes everyone can agree on. Help your family plan, shop for, and prepare your climate-friendly meals.

Learn More

BOOKS

Collins, Anna. *Climate Change Crisis*. New York, NY: Lucent Press, 2019.

Labrecque, Ellen. *Climate Change*. Ann Arbor, MI: Cherry Lake Publishing, 2017.

Hirsch, Rebecca E. *Climate Scientists at Work*. Vero Beach, FL: Rourke Educational Media, 2019.

WEBSITES

Carbon Footprint Calculator
https://www3.epa.gov/carbon-footprint-calculator

Climate Change
https://kids.nationalgeographic.com/explore/science/climate-change

NASA Climate Kids
https://climatekids.nasa.gov

BIBLIOGRAPHY

European Commission. "Causes of Climate Change." Last modified June 28, 2017. https://ec.europa.eu/clima/change/causes_en

NASA Earth Observatory. "World of Change: Global Temperatures." https://earthobservatory.nasa.gov/world-of-change/DecadalTemp

NASA Global Climate Change. "Facts." Last modified December 13, 2019. https://climate.nasa.gov/vital-signs/sea-level

Our World in Data. "CO_2 and Greenhouse Gas Emissions." Last modified December 2019. https://ourworldindata.org/co2-and-other-greenhouse-gas-emissions

UN Environment. "UN Environment's 2018 Emissions Gap Report." https://www.unenvironment.org/interactive/emissions-gap-report

GLOSSARY

albedo (al-BEE-doh) a measurement of how much an object or area reflects light

atmosphere (AT-muhss-feer) the layer of gases that surrounds Earth

biofuels (BYE-yo-fyoolz) materials made from animal waste or plants that humans can use as fuel

correlation (KOR-uh-lay-shuhn) a connection between two or more things that change in sync

deforestation (di-for-eh-STAY-shuhn) the removal of all the trees in an area

extinct (ek-STINGT) no longer existing on Earth

fossil fuels (FAH-suhl FYOOLZ) materials that form naturally over millions of years and that can be used as fuels

hydrologic cycle (hai-druh-LAH-jik SAI-kul) also known as the water cycle; the circulation of water through the oceans, atmosphere, and land, made possible by evaporation and precipitation

ocean acidification (OH-shun ah-sid-if-i-KAY-shun) a change in ocean water to become more acidic due to extra carbon dioxide in the air

precipitation (pruh-sip-i-TAY-shuhn) the water that falls from clouds to the ground; rain, snow, and hail are forms of precipitation

INDEX

ABOUT THE AUTHOR

Renae Gilles is an author, editor, and ecologist from the Pacific Northwest. She has a bachelor's degree in humanities from Evergreen State College and a master's in biology from Eastern Washington University. Renae and her husband live in Washington with their two daughters, Edith and Louisa.